I0011478

Book 1
Android Programming In a Day!
BY SAM KEY

&

Book 2
Ruby Programming Professional Made Easy
BY SAM KEY

Book 1
Android Programming In a Day!

BY SAM KEY

The Power Guide for Beginners In Android App Programming

Programming Box Set #77: Android Programming in a Day & Ruby Programming Professional Made Easy

Programming Box Set #77: Android Programming in a Day & Ruby Programming Professional Made Easy

Table Of Contents

Introduction

I want to thank you and congratulate you for purchasing the book, "Introduction to Android Programming in a Day – The Power Guide for Beginners in Android App Programming".

This book contains proven steps and strategies on how to get started with Android app development.

This book will focus on preparing you with the fun and tiring world of Android app development. Take note that this book will not teach you on how to program. It will revolve around the familiarization of the Android SDK and Eclipse IDE.

Why not focus on programming immediately? Unfortunately, the biggest reason many aspiring Android developers stop on learning this craft is due to the lack of wisdom on the Android SDK and Eclipse IDE.

Sure, you can also make apps using other languages like Python and other IDEs on the market. However, you can expect that it is much more difficult than learning Android's SDK and Eclipse's IDE.

On the other hand, you can use tools online to develop your Android app for you. But where's the fun in that? You will not learn if you use such tools. Although it does not mean that you should completely stay away from that option.

Anyway, the book will be split into four chapters. The first will prepare you and tell you the things you need before you develop apps. The second will tell you how you can configure your project. The third will introduce you to the Eclipse IDE. And the last chapter will teach you on how to run your program in your Android device.

Also, this book will be sprinkled with tidbits about the basic concepts of Android app development. And as you read along, you will have an idea on what to do next.

Thanks again for purchasing this book, I hope you enjoy it!

Chapter 1: Preparation

Android application development is not easy. You must have some decent background in program development. It is a plus if you know Visual Basic and Java. And it will be definitely a great advantage if you are familiar or have already used Eclipse's IDE (Integrated Development Environment). Also, being familiar with XML will help you.

You will need a couple of things before you can start developing apps.

First, you will need a high-end computer. It is common that other programming development kits do not need a powerful computer in order to create applications. However, creating programs for Android is a bit different. You will need more computing power for you to run Android emulators, which are programs that can allow you to test your programs in your computer.

Using a weak computer without a decent processor and a good amount of RAM will only make it difficult for you to run those emulators. If you were able to run it, it will run slowly.

Second, you will need an Android device. That device will be your beta tester. With it, you will know how your program will behave in an Android device. When choosing the test device, make sure that it is at par with the devices of the market you are targeting for your app. If you are targeting tablet users, use a tablet. If you are targeting smartphones, then use a smartphone.

Third, you will need the Android SDK (Software Development Kit) from Google. The SDK is a set of files and programs that can allow you to create and compile your program's code. As of this writing, the latest Android SDK's file size is around 350mb. It will take you 15 – 30 minutes to download it. If you uncompressed the Android SDK file, it will take up around 450mb of your computer's disk space. The link to the download page is: http://developer.android.com/sdk/index.html

The SDK can run on Windows XP, Windows 7, Mac OSX 10.8.5 (or higher), and Linux distros that can run 32bit applications and has glibc (GNU C library) 2.11 or higher.

Once you have unpacked the contents of the file you downloaded, open the SDK Manager. That program is the development kit's update tool. To make sure you have the latest versions of the kit's components, run the manager once in a while and download those updates. Also, you can use the SDK Manager to download older versions of SDK. You must do that in case you want to make programs with devices with dated Android operating systems.

Chapter 2: Starting Your First Project

To start creating programs, you will need to open Eclipse. The Eclipse application file can be found under the eclipse folder on the extracted files from the Android SDK. Whenever you run Eclipse, it will ask you where you want your Eclipse workspace will be stored. You can just use the default location and just toggle the don't show checkbox.

New Project

To start a new Android application project, just click on the dropdown button of the New button on Eclipse's toolbar. A context menu will appear, and click on the Android application project.

The New Android Application project details window will appear. In there, you will need to input some information for your project. You must provide your program's application name, project name, and package name. Also, you can configure the minimum and target SDK where your program can run and the SDK that will be used to compile your code. And lastly, you can indicate the default theme that your program will use.

Application Name

The application name will be the name that will be displayed on the Google's Play Store when you post it there. The project name will be more of a file name for Eclipse. It will be the project's identifier. It should be unique for every project that you build in Eclipse. By default, Eclipse will generate a project and package name for your project when you type something in the Application Name text box.

Package Name

The package name is not usually displayed for users. Take note that in case you will develop a large program, you must remember that your package name should never be changed. On the other hand, it is common that package names are the reverse of your domain name plus your project's name. For example, if your website's domain name is www.mywebsite.com and your project's name is Hello World, a good package name for your project will be com.mywebsite.helloworld.

The package name should follow the Java package name convention. The naming convention is there to prevent users from having similar names, which could result to numerous conflicts. Some of the rules you need to follow for the package name are:

- Your package name should be all in lower caps. Though Eclipse will accept a package name with a capital letter, but it is still best to adhere to standard practice.
- The reverse domain naming convention is included as a standard practice.
- Avoid using special characters in the package name. Instead, you can replace it with underscores.
- Also, you should never use or include the default com.example in your package name. Google Play will not accept an app with a package name like that.

Minimum SDK

Minimum required SDK could be set to lower or the lowest version of Android. Anything between the latest and the set minimum required version can run your program. Setting it to the lowest, which is API 1 or Android 1.0, can make your target audience wider.

Setting it to Android 2.2 (Froyo) or API 8, can make your program run on almost 95% of all Android devices in the world. The drawback fn this is that the features you can include in your program will be limited. Adding new features will force your minimum required SDK to move higher since some of the new functions in Android is not available on lower versions of the API (Application Programming Interface).

Target SDK

The target SDK should be set to the version of Android that most of your target audience uses. It indicates that you have tested your program to that version. And it means that your program is fully functional if they use it on a device that runs the target Android version.

Whenever a new version of Android appears, you should also update the target SDK of your program. Of course, before you release it to the market again, make sure that you test it on an updated device.

If a device with the same version as your set target SDK runs your program, it will not do any compatibility behavior or adjust itself to run the program. By default, you should set it to the highest version to attract your potential app buyers. Setting a lower version for your target SDK would make your program old and dated. By the way, the target SDK should be always higher or equal with the minimum target SDK version.

Compile with

The compile with version should be set to the latest version of Android. This is to make sure that your program will run on almost all versions down to the minimum version you have indicated, and to take advantage of the newest features and optimization offered by the latest version of Android. By default, the Android SDK will only have one version available for this option, which is API 20 or Android 4.4 (KitKat Wear).

After setting those all up, it is time to click on the Next button. The new page in the screen will contain some options such as creating custom launcher icon and creating activity. As of now, you do not need to worry about those. Just leave the default values and check, and click the Next button once again.

Custom Launcher Icon

Since you have left the Create Custom Launcher option checked, the next page will bring you in the launcher icon customization page. In there, you will be given three options on how you would create your launcher. Those options are launcher icons made from an image, clipart, or text.

With the text and clipart method, you can easily create an icon you want without thinking about the size and quality of the launcher icon. With those two, you can just get a preset image from the SDK or Android to use as a launcher icon. The same goes with the text method since all you need is to type the letters you want to appear on the icon and the SDK will generate an icon based on that.

The launcher icon editor also allows you to change the background and foreground color of your icon. Also, you can scale the text and clipart by changing the value of the additional padding of the icon. And finally, you can add simple 3D shapes on your icon to make it appear more professional.

Bitmap Iconography Tips

When it comes to images, you need to take note of a few reminders. First, always make sure that you will use vector images. Unlike the typical bitmap images (pictures taken from cameras or images created using Paint), vector images provide accurate and sharp images. You can scale it multiple times, but its sharpness will not disappear and will not pixelate. After all, vector images do not contain information about pixels. It only has numbers and location of the colors and lines that will appear in it. When it is scaled, it does not perform antialiasing or stretching since its image will be mathematically rendered.

In case that you will be the one creating or designing the image that you will use for your program and you will be creating a bitmap image, make sure that you start with a large image. A large image is easier to create and design.

Also, since in Android, multiple sizes of your icon will be needed, a large icon can make it easier for you to make smaller ones. Take note that if you scale a big picture into a small one, some details will be lost, but it will be easier to edit and fix and it will still look crisp. On the other hand, if you scale a small image into a big one, it will pixelate and insert details that you do not intend to show such as jagged and blurred edges.

Nevertheless, even when scaling down a big image into a smaller one, do not forget to rework the image. Remember that a poor-looking icon makes people think that the app you are selling is low-quality. And again, if you do not want to go through all that, create a vector image instead.

Also, when you create an image, make sure that it will be visible in any background. Aside from that, it is advisable to make it appear uniform with other Android icons. To do that, make sure that your image has a distinct silhouette that will make it look like a 3D image. The icon should appear as if you were looking above it and as if the source of light is on top of the image. The topmost part of the icon should appear lighter and the bottom part should appear darker.

Activity

Once you are done with your icon, click on the Next button. The page will now show the Activity window. It will provide you with activity templates to work on. The window has a preview box where you can see what your app will look like for every activity template. Below the selection, there is a description box that will tell you what each template does. For now, select the Blank Activity and click Next. The next page will ask you some details regarding the activity. Leave it on its default values and click Finish.

Once you do that, Eclipse will setup your new project. It might take a lot of time, especially if you are using a dated computer. The next chapter will discuss the programming interface of Eclipse.

Chapter 3: Getting Familiar with Eclipse and Contents of an Android App

When Eclipse has finished its preparation, you will be able to start doing something to your program. But hold onto your horses; explore Eclipse first before you start fiddling with anything.

Editing Area

In the middle of the screen, you will see a preview of your program. In it, you will see your program's icon beside the title of your program. Just left of it is the palette window. It contains all the elements that you can place in your program.

Both of these windows are inside Eclipse's editing area. You will be spending most of your time here, especially if you are going to edit or view something in your code or layout.

The form widgets tab will be expanded in the palette by default. There you will see the regular things you see in an Android app such as buttons, radio buttons, progress bar (the circle icon that spins when something is loading in your device or the bar the fills up when your device is loading), seek bar, and the ratings bar (the stars you see in reviews).

Aside from the form widgets, there are other elements that you can check and use. Press the horizontal tabs or buttons and examine all the elements you can possibly use in your program.

To insert a widget in your program, you can just drag the element you want to include from the palette and drop it in your program's preview. Eclipse will provide you visual markers and grid snaps for you to place the widgets you want on the exact place you want. Easy, right?

Take note, some of the widgets on the palette may require higher-level APIs or versions of Android. For example, the Grid Layout from the Layouts section of the palette requires API 14 (Android 4.0 Ice Cream Sandwich) or higher. If you add it in your program, it will ask you if you want to install it. In case you did include and install it, remember that it will not be compatible for older versions or any device running on API 13 and lower. It is advisable that you do not include any element that asks for installation. It might result into errors.

Output Area, Status Bar, and Problem Browser

On the bottom part of Eclipse, the status bar, problem browser, and output area can be found. It will contain messages regarding to the state of your project. If Eclipse found errors in your program, it will be listed there. Always check the Problems bar for any issues. Take note that you cannot run or compile your program if Eclipse finds at least one error on your project.

Navigation Pane

On the leftmost part of your screen is the navigation pane that contains the package explorer. The package explorer lets you browse all the files that are included in your project. Three of the most important files that you should know where to look for are:

- activity_main.xml: This file is your program's main page or window. And it will be the initial file that will be opened when you create a new project. In case you accidentally close it on your editor window, you can find it at: YourProjectName > res > layout > activity_main.xml.

- MainActivity.java: As of now, you will not need to touch this file. However, it is important to know where it is since later in your Android development activities, you will need to understand it and its contents. It is located at: YourProjectName > src > YourPackageName > MainActivity.java.

- AndroidManifest.xml: It contains the essential information that you have set up a while ago when you were creating your project file in Eclipse. You can edit the minimum and target SDK in there. It is located at YourProjectName > AndroidManifest.xml.

Aside from those files, you should take note of the following directories:

- src/: This is where most of your program's source files will be placed. And your main activity file is locafile is located.

- res/: Most of the resources will be placed here. The resources are placed inside the subdirectories under this folder.

- res/drawable-hdpi/: Your high density bitmap files that you might show in your app will go in here.

- res/layout/: All the pages or interface in your app will be located here – including your activity_main.xml.

- res/values/: The values you will store and use in your program will be placed in this directory in form of XML files.

In the event that you will create multiple projects, remember that the directory for those other projects aside from the one you have opened will still be available in your package explorer. Because of that, you might get confused over the files you are working on. Thankfully, Eclipse's title bar indicates the location and name of the file you are editing, which makes it easier to know what is currently active on the editing area.

Outline Box

Displays the current structure of the file you are editing. The outline panel will help you visualize the flow and design of your app. Also, it can help you find the widgets you want to edit.

Properties Box

Whenever you are editing a layout file, the properties box will appear below the outline box. With the properties box, you can edit certain characteristics of a widget. For example, if you click on the Hello World text on the preview of your main activity layout file, the contents of the properties box will be populated. In there, you can edit the properties of the text element that you have clicked. You can change the text, height, width, and even its font color.

Menu and Toolbar

The menu bar contains all the major functionalities of Eclipse. In case you do not know where the button of a certain tool is located, you can just invoke that tool's function on the menu bar. On the other hand, the tool bar houses all the major functions in Eclipse. The most notable buttons there are the New, Save, and Run.

As of now, look around Eclipse's interface. Also, do not do or change anything on the main activity file or any other file. The next chapter will discuss about how to run your program. As of now, the initial contents of your project are also valid as an android program. Do not change anything since you might produce an unexpected error. Nevertheless, if you really do want to change something, go ahead. You can just create another project for you to keep up with the next chapter.

Chapter 4: Running Your Program

By this time, even if you have not done anything yet to your program, you can already run and test it in your Android device or emulator. Why teach this first before the actual programming? Well, unlike typical computer program development, Android app development is a bit bothersome when it comes to testing.

First, the program that you are developing is intended for Android devices. You cannot actually run it normally in your computer without the help of an emulator. And you will actually do a lot of testing. Even with the first lines of code or changes in your program, you will surely want to test it.

Second, the Android emulator works slow. Even with good computers, the emulator that comes with the Android SDK is painstakingly sluggish. Alternatively, you can use BlueStacks. BlueStacks is a free Android emulator that works better than the SDK's emulator. It can even run games with it! However, it is buggy and does not work well (and does not even run sometimes) with every computer.

This chapter will focus on running your program into your Android device. You will need to have a USB data cable and connect your computer and Android. Also, you will need to have the right drivers for your device to work as a testing platform for the programs you will develop. Unfortunately, this is the preferred method for most beginners since running your app on Android emulators can bring a lot more trouble since it is super slow. And that might even discourage you to continue Android app development.

Why Android Emulators are Slow

Why are Android emulators slow? Computers can run virtual OSs without any problems, but why cannot the Android emulator work fine? Running virtual OSs is not something as resource-extensive anymore with today's computer standards. However, with Android, you will actually emulate an OS together with a mobile device. And nowadays, these mobile devices are as powerful as some of the dated computers back then. Regular computers will definitely have a hard time with that kind of payload from an Android emulator.

USB Debugging Mode

To run your program in an Android device, connect your Android to your computer. After that, set your Android into USB debugging mode. Depending on the version of the Android device you are using, the steps might change.

For 3.2 and older Android devices:

Go to Settings > Applications > Development

For 4.0 and newer Android devices:

Go to Settings > Developer Options

For 4.2 and newer Android devices with hidden Developer Options:

Go to Settings > About Phone. After that, tap the Build Number seven times. Go back to the previous screen. The Developer Options should be visible now.

Android Device Drivers

When USB debugging is enabled, your computer will install the right drivers for the Android device that you have. If your computer does not have the right drivers, you will not be able to run your program on your device. If that happens to you, visit this page: http://developer.android.com/tools/extras/oem-usb.html. It contains instructions on how you can install the right driver for your device and operating system.

Running an App in Your Android Device Using Eclipse

Once your device is already connected and you have the right drivers for it, you can now do a test run of your application. On your Eclipse window, click the Run button on the toolbar or in the menu bar.

If a Run As window appeared, select the Android Application option and click on the OK button. After that, a dialog box will appear. It will provide you with two options: running the program on an Android device or on an AVD (Android Virtual Device) or emulator.

If your device was properly identified by your computer, it will appear on the list. Click on your device's name and click OK. Eclipse will compile your Android app, install it on your device, and then run it. That is how simple it is.

Take note, there will be times that your device will appear offline on the list. In case that happens, there are two simple fixes that you can do to make it appear online again: restart your device or disable and enable the USB debugging function on your device.

Now, you can start placing widgets on your main activity file. However, always make sure that you do not place any widgets that require higher APIs.

Conclusion

Thank you again for purchasing this book!

I hope this book was able to help you get started with Android Programming in a Day!.

The next step is to study the following:

View and Viewgroups: View and Viewgroups are the two types of objects that you will be dealing with Android. View objects are the elements or widgets that you see in Android programs. Viewgroup objects act as containers to those View objects.

Relative, Linear, and Table Layout: When it comes to designing your app, you need to know the different types of layouts. In later versions of Android, you can use other versions of layouts, but of course, the API requirements will go up if you use them. Master these, and you will be able to design faster and cleaner.

Adding Activities or Interface: Of course, you would not want your program to contain one page only. You need more. You must let your app customers to see more content and functions. In order to do that, you will need to learn adding activities to your program. This is the part when developing your Android app will be tricky. You will not be able to rely completely on the drag and drop function and graphical layout view of Eclipse. You will need to start typing some code into your program.

Adding the Action Bar: The action bar is one of the most useful elements in Android apps. It provides the best location for the most used functions in your program. And it also aid your users when switching views, tabs, or drop down list.

Once you have gain knowledge on those things, you will be able to launch a decent app on the market. The last thing you might want to do is to learn how to make your program support other Android devices.

You must know very well that Android devices come in all shapes and form. An Android device can be a tablet, a smartphone, or even a television. Also, they come with different screen sizes. You cannot just expect that all your customers will be using a 4-inch display smartphone. Also, you should think about the versions of Android they are using. Lastly, you must also add language options to your programs. Even though English is fine, some users will appreciate if your program caters to the primary language that they use.

And that is about it for this book. Make sure you do not stop learning Android app development.

Finally, if you enjoyed this book, please take the time to share your thoughts and post a review on Amazon. We do our best to reach out to readers and provide the best value we can. Your positive review will help us achieve that. It'd be greatly appreciated!

Thank you and good luck!

Book 2
Ruby Programming Professional Made Easy

BY SAM KEY

Expert Ruby Programming Language Success in a Day for any Computer User

Programming Box Set #77: Android Programming in a Day & Ruby Programming Professional Made Easy

Table Of Contents

Introduction

I want to thank you and congratulate you for purchasing the book, *"Professional Ruby Programming Made Easy: Expert Ruby Programming Language Success in a Day for Any Computer User!"*

This book contains proven steps and strategies on how to write basic lines of code in Ruby. This is especially made for amateur programmers with little to no experience in coding.

Ruby is a programming language which people think is ideal for newbies in the programming field. Congratulations on choosing this programming language. In this book, you will be introduced to all the fundamental aspects of coding in Ruby.

This book will give you a huge boost in your programming skills. However, it is also important to quickly supplement yourself with advanced Ruby tutorials after you are done with this book to retain the knowledge you gain from it.

Thanks again for purchasing this book, I hope you enjoy it!

Chapter 1: Setting Up

This book will assume that you are a bit familiar with computer programming and have made a few lines of codes in some languages. Also, from time to time, the book will provide further explanation of terms and methods that can easily confuse new programmers. In case you encounter a foreign term in the discussion, just take note of it since it and other such terms will be discussed later.

Before anything else, get the latest stable version of Ruby from the web. As of this writing, Ruby's stable version is 2.1.5.

Go to https://www.ruby-lang.org/en/documentation/installation/. In there, you can get the right installer package for the operating system that your computer is running on.

Be mindful of what you are going to download. Many people tend to download the source code of Ruby instead of the installation packages.

Take note of the location or directory where you will install Ruby. Once you are done with the installation, open Ruby's interactive shell.

For people who are using a computer running on Windows, you will find the interactive interpreter inside the bin folder located inside your Ruby installation folder. The file is named irb.bat. If you have installed Ruby using the default location, the interactive shell will be located at: "c:\Ruby21\bin\irb.bat".

What is the interactive shell anyway? In Ruby, you can program using two modes: the interactive mode and the programming mode.

Ruby's Interactive Mode

The interactive mode is an environment wherein Ruby will provide immediate feedback in every line of code or statement you type in to it. It is an ideal environment where new Ruby programmers can test and experiment with codes quickly. You will be using this mode in most parts of this book.

The interactive mode or shell will appear like a typical console or command prompt. In the shell, you should be familiar with two things. First is the cursor. Second is the prompt.

The cursor indicates where you can type or if you can type anything. In the interpreter shell, you can use overtype mode on this by pressing the insert key on your keyboard. You can return to insert mode by pressing the insert key again.

The prompt will look like this: irb(main):001:0>. If this prompt is on, it means that Ruby is ready to accept a line of code or statement from you. For now, type a letter a in the prompt and press the Enter key. The shell or interpreter will move the cursor, show a bunch of text, and display the prompt once again:

```
irb(main):001:0> a
NameError: undefined local variable or method 'a' for main:Object
        from (irb):1
        from C:/Ruby21/bin/irb:11:in '<main>'
irb(main):002:0>
```

This time, type "a" on the shell and then press the Enter key. Instead of an error, you have received => "a". Now, type "1" without the quotes. Just like before, the interpreter just provided you with a reply containing the number you entered.

Why does the letter a without the quotes returned an error? As you can see, Ruby provided you with an error message when you just entered the letter a without quotes. In Ruby, characters enclosed in double or single quotes are treated differently.

In the case of the letter a, Ruby understood that when you input "a" with the quotes, you meant that you are inputting the letter a. On the other hand, Ruby thought of something else when you input the letter a without the quotes, which will be discussed later.

You will receive error messages like the one before or other variations of it if you input something that violates Ruby's syntax or something that is impossible to be evaluated or executed by the interpreter. In simple terms, Ruby will provide you notifications like that if it does not understand what you said or cannot do what you commanded.

Now, type "1 + 1", without the double quotes, and press the Enter key. Instead of an error, you will receive this instead:

```
=> 2
```

Every time you press the Enter key, the shell check the command or statement you created. If it does not violate the syntax, it will proceed on checking if every word and symbols you placed make sense. Once the statement passes that check, it will evaluate and execute the statement and provide a result or feedback.

In this case, Ruby has evaluated the addition operation you commanded and replied the number 2, which is the sum of 1 + 1. Just before the number 2, an equal sign and "greater than" sign were placed. Those two denotes that the next value is the result of the statement you entered.

You might have thought that Ruby can be a good calculator. Indeed it is, but statements like "1 + 1" and "a" are only processed like that in the interactive mode of Ruby. If you include a line like that when coding in programming mode, you will certainly encounter a syntax error.

Ruby's Programming Mode

On the other hand, the programming mode is a method wherein you can execute blocks of code in one go. You will need to type the code of your program first before you can run and see what it will do.

You will need a text editor to type your program. Any simple text editor such as Notepad in Windows is sufficient for programming Ruby. However, to reduce typos and keyword mistakes, it is advisable that you use a source code editor, which will provide you with syntax highlighting and checking. In Windows users, a few of the best source code editors you can use for Ruby programming are Notepad++, TextWrangler, JEdit, and Crimson Editor.

Once you are done typing your code, save it as a .rb file. For Windows users: if you have let Ruby associate .rb and .rbw files to it, all .rb files or Ruby code you have created can be opened by just double clicking on them. They will act as if they are typical Windows program.

By the way, programming mode does not provide instant reply to your expressions. For example, if you input a = 1 + 1 in interactive mode, it will reply with => 2. In programming mode, that statement will not provide any output.

Also, if one of the lines encounters an error, the program will stop executing the next lines after the line that generated the error.

Chapter 2: Ruby Syntax

In the first chapter, you have encountered your first syntax error. For those who are not familiar with the term syntax, syntax is a set of 'language' rules that you must follow in order for a programming language (in this case, Ruby) to understand you.

A programming language's syntax is similar to English grammar where you need to correctly arrange parts of the sentence—such as verbs, nouns, and adjectives—to make it coherent and grammatically correct.

The two major differences between Ruby's syntax (or other programming languages' syntax as well) and English's set of grammar rules are Ruby's syntax's strictness and inflexibility. It is set to behave like that because computers, unlike humans, cannot understand or comprehend context. Also, if computers understand context and programming languages' syntaxes become lax, computer programming will become difficult.

First, computer will become prone to misunderstanding or misinterpreting your statements. If you point to a jar of jam in a shelf full of jars and requested people to get the one you want, most of them will surely get and give you the wrong jar. That kind of situation will happen if a programming language's syntax became loose.

Here are some of Ruby's syntax rules:

Whitespace

Whitespace (continuous spaces and tabs) are ignored in Ruby code unless they are placed inside strings. For example, the expression "1 + 1", "1   + 1", or 1+1 will provide the same result in Ruby.

Line Ending Terminators

New lines and semicolons are treated as line endings. Ruby works by reading your program's lines one by one. Each line is considered a statement. A statement is a combination of keywords, operators, values, methods, and properties, which is translated as a command.

Every time you put a semicolon or move to the next line, the previous line will be treated as a statement. There are some cases that if you do not place a semicolon but used a new line character (the one that the Enter key produces and pushes the cursor to move to the next line) to write a new line of code will make Ruby think that the previous line and the new line of code is just one statement. For example:

```
irb(main):001:0> 1 +
irb(main):002:0* 1 +
irb(main):003:0*
```

If you typed that in Ruby's interactive mode, you will not encounter an error or reply from Ruby. Instead, it allowed you to move on to the next line and type another line of code.

If you have noticed, the greater than sign at the end of the prompt changed into an asterisk. The asterisk denotes that all the succeeding lines of code after the previous one will be treated as one statement in Ruby or the next lines are meant to be continuations of the previous line.

Ruby behaved like that since you left an operator at the end of the line and did not place a value on the operator's right hand side. So, Ruby is treating the example as 1 + 1 +. If you place another 1 at the last line, Ruby will interpret that 1 as the last value to your expression and evaluate it. It will then produce a reply, which is => 3.

Case Sensitivity

Identifiers or names of constants, variables, and methods in Ruby are case sensitive. For example, a variable named Variable1 is different from variable1.

Comments

In computer languages, comments are used to serve as markers, reminders, or explanations within the program. Comments are ignored by Ruby and are not executed like regular statements.

Some convert statements in order to disable them. It is handy during debugging or testing alternate statements to get what they want since deleting a statement may make them forget it after a few minutes of coding another line.

To create comments in Ruby, use the hash sign (#) to let Ruby know that the succeeding characters is a comment line. You can insert comments at the end of statements. For example:

```
irb(main):001:0> #This is a comment.
irb(main):002:0* 1 + 1
=> 2
irb(main):003:0> 1 + 1 #This is a comment.
=> 2
irb(main):003:0>
```

As you can see, the line after the hash sign was just ignored and Ruby just evaluated the expression 1 + 1.

In case you are going to start programming using Ruby's programming mode, there will be times that you will want to create multiple lines of comments. You can still use hash signs to create multiple lines. For example:

```
#This is a comment.
#This is another comment.
#This is the last comment.
```

If you do not want to use that method, you can do this by using the =begin and =end keyword. Below is an example on how to use them:

```
=begin
This is a comment
```

```
This is another comment.
This is the last comment.
=end
```

All lines after the =begin and before the =end keyword will be treated as comment lines.

Those are just the primary rules in Ruby's syntax. Some commands have syntax of their own. They will be discussed together with the commands themselves.

Chapter 3: Parts of a Statement

You have been seeing the term statement in the previous chapters. As mentioned before, a statement is a combination of keywords, operators, variables, constants, values, expressions, methods, and properties which is translated as a command.

In this chapter, you will know what six of those parts are: variables, constants, keywords, values, operators, and expressions. Let's start with variables.

Variables

In Math, you know that variables are placeholders for values. For example:

x = 1 + 1

x = 2

y = 3

In the previous line, variable x has a value of 2 and variable y has a value of 3. Variables in Ruby (or other programming languages) act the same way – as placeholders. However, unlike in Math, variables in Ruby do not act as placeholders for numbers alone. It can contain different types of values like strings and objects.

To create variables in Ruby, all you need is to assign a value to one. For example:

irb(main):001:0> a = 12

That example commands Ruby to create a variable named a and assign the number 12 as its value. To check the value of a variable in Ruby's interpreter mode, input a on a new line and press the Enter key. It will produce the result:

=> 12

A while ago, instead of getting a reply like that from Ruby, you have got this instead:

```
NameError: undefined local variable or method 'a' for main:Object
    from (irb):1
    from C:/Ruby21/bin/irb:11:in '<main>'
```

Technically, the error means that Ruby was not able to find a variable or method with the name a. Now, when you input a, it does not produce that error anymore since you have already created a variable named a.

By the name, in computer programming, the names you give to variables and other entities in the program are called identifiers. Some call them IDs or tokens instead.

There are some set of rules when giving an identifier to a variable. Identifiers can contain letters, numbers, and underscores. A variable identifier must start with a lower case letter or an underscore. It may also contain one or more characters. Also, variable identifiers should not be the same with a keyword or reserved words.

Just like any programming languages, reserved or special keywords cannot be used as identifiers.

Constants

Constants are like variables, but you can only assign a value to them once in your program and their identifiers must start with an uppercase letter. Reassigning a value to them will generate an error or a warning.

Keywords

Keywords are special reserved words in Ruby that perform specific functions and commands. Some of them are placeholder for special values such as true, false, and nil.

The nil value means that the entity that contains it does not have a value. To put it simply, all variables will have the nil value if no value was assigned to it. When they are used and they have nil as their value, Ruby will return a warning if the –w is on.

Values

In Ruby, there are multiple types of values that you can assign in a variable. In programming, they are called literals. In coding Ruby, you will be dealing with these literals every time.

Integers

You can write integers in four forms or numeral systems: decimal, hexadecimal, octal, and binary. To make Ruby understand that you are declaring integers in hexadecimal (base 16), octal (base 8), or binary (base 2), you should use prefixes or leading signs.

If you are going to use octal, use 0 (zero). If you are going to use hexadecimal, use 0x (zero-x). If you are going to use binary, use 0b (zero-b). If you are going to use decimal, there is no need for any optional leading signs.

Depending on the size of the integer, it can be categorized in the class Fixnum or Bignum.

Floating Numbers

Any integer with decimals is considered a floating number. All floating numbers are under the class Float.

Strings

Strings are values inside single or double quotation marks. They are treated as text in Ruby. You can place expression evaluation inside strings without terminating your quotes. You can just insert expressions by using the hash sign and enclosing the expression using curly braces. For example:

```
irb(main):001:0> a = "the sum of 3 and 1 is: #{3 + 1}."
=> "the sum of 3 and 1 is: 4."
```

You can also access variables or constants in Ruby and include them in a string by placing a hash sign (#) before the variable or constant's name. For example:

irb(main):001:0> b = "string inside variable."
=> "string inside variable."
irb(main):002:0> b = "You can access a #{b}"
=> "You can access a string inside variable."

Arrays

An array is a data type that can contain multiple data or values. Creating arrays in Ruby is simple. Type Array and then follow it with values enclosed inside square brackets. Make sure that you separate each value with a comma. Any exceeding commas will be ignored and will not generate error. For example:

irb(main):001:0> arraysample = Array[1, 2, 3]
=> [1, 2, 3]

To access a value of an array, you must use its index. The index of an array value depends on its location in the array. For example, the value 2 in the arraysample variable has an index number of 0. The value 2, has an index of 1. And the value 3, has an index of 2. The index increments by 1 and starts with zero.

Below is an example on how to access a value in an array:

irb(main):001:0> arraysample[2]
=> 3

Hashes or Associative Arrays:

Hashes are arrays that contain paired keys (named index) and values. Instead of a numbered index, you can assign and use keys to access your array values.

irb(main):001:0> hashsample = Hash["First" => 1, "Second" = > 2]
=> {"First"=>1, "Second"=>2]

To access a hash value, you just need to call it using its key instead of an index number. For example:

irb(main):001:0> hashsample["Second"]
=> 2

Expressions

Expressions are combinations of operators, variables, values, and/or keywords. Expressions result into a value or can be evaluated by Ruby. A good example of an expression is 1 + 1. In that, Ruby can evaluate that expression and it will result to 2. The plus sign (+) is one of many operators in Ruby.

You can assign expression to a variable. The result of the expression will be stored on the variable instead of the expression itself. For example:

irb(main):001:0> a = 1 + 1
=> 2

If you check the value of a by inputting a into the shell, it will return 2 not 1 + 1.

As mentioned a while ago, expressions can also contain variables. If you assign a simple or complex expression with a variable to another variable, Ruby will handle all the evaluation. For example:

irb(main):001:0> a = 2
=> 2
irb(main):002:0> b = 4
=> 4
irb(main):003:0> c = a + b + 6
=> 12

Operators

Operators are symbols or keywords that command the computer to perform operations or evaluations. Ruby's operators are not limited to performing arithmetic operations alone. The following are the operators you can use in Ruby:

Arithmetic Operators

Arithmetic operators allow Ruby to evaluate simple Math expressions. They are: + for addition, - for subtraction, * for multiplication, / for division, % for modulus, and ** for exponent.

Division in Ruby works differently. If you are dividing integers, you will get an integer quotient. If the quotient should have a fractional component or decimal on it, they will be removed. For example:

```
irb(main):001:0> 5 / 2
=> 2
```

If you want to get an accurate quotient with a fractional component, you must perform division with fractional components For example:

```
irb(main):001:0> 5.0 / 2
=> 2.5
```

For those who are unfamiliar with modulus: modulus performs regular division and returns the remainder instead of the quotient. For example:

```
irb(main):001:0> 5 % 2
=> 1
```

Comparison Operators

Ruby can compare numbers, too, with the help of comparison operators. Comparison operations provide two results only: true or false. For example:

```
irb(main):001:0> 1 > 2
=> false
```

The value 1 is less than 2, but not greater than; therefore, Ruby evaluated that the expression is false.

Other comparison operators that you can use in Ruby are: == for has equal value, != for does not have equal value, > for greater than, < for less than, >= for greater than or equal, and <= for less than or equal. There four other comparison operators (===, <=>, .eql?, and .equal?) in Ruby, but you do not need them for now.

Assignment Operators

Assignment operators are used to assign value to operators, properties, and other entities in Ruby. You have already encountered the most used assignment operator, which is the equal sign (=). There are other assignment operators other than that, which are simple combination of the assignment operator (=) and arithmetic operators.

They are += for add and assign, -= for subtract and assign, *= for multiply and assign, /= for divide and assign, % for modulus and assign, and ** for raise and assign.

All of them perform the arithmetic operation and the values they use are the value of the entity on their left and the expression on their right first before assigning the result of the operation to the entity on its left. It might seem confusing, so here is an example:

```
irb(main):001:0> a = 1
=> 1
irb(main):002:0> a += 2
=> 3
```

In the example, variable a was given a value of 1. On the next statement, the add and assign operator was used. After the operation, a's value became 3 because a + 2 = 3. That can also be achieved by doing this:

```
irb(main):001:0> a = 1
=> 1
irb(main):002:0> a = a + 2
```

=> 3

If the value to the right of these operators is an expression that contain multiple values and operators, it will be evaluated first before the assignment operators perform their operations. For example:

```
irb(main):001:0> a = 1
=> 1
irb(main):002:0> a += 3 * 2
=> 7
```

The expression 3 * 2 was evaluated first, which resulted to 6. Then six was added to variable a that had a value of 1, which resulted to 7. And that value value was assigned to variable a.

Other Operators

As you advance your Ruby programming skills, you will encounter more operators. And they are:

Logical Operator: and, or, &&, ||, !, not
Defined Operator: defined?
Reference Operators: ., ::

Chapter 4: Object Oriented Programming

In the previous chapters, you have learned the basics of Ruby programming. Those chapters also serve as your introduction to computer programming since most programming languages follow the same concepts and have similar entities in them. In this chapter, you will learn why some programmers love Ruby.

Ruby is an Object Oriented Programming (OOP) language. Object oriented programming makes use of objects and classes. Those objects and classes can be reused which in turn makes it easier to code programs that require multiple instances of values that are related to each other.

Programming methods can be categorized into two: Procedural and Object Oriented. If you have experienced basic programming before, you mostly have experienced procedural instead of object oriented.

In procedural, your program's code revolves around actions. For example, you have a program that prints what a user will input. It is probable that your program's structure will be as simple as take user input, assign the input to a variable, and then print the content of the variable. As you can see, procedural is a straightforward forward method.

Classes and Objects

Classes are like templates for objects. For example, a Fender Telecaster and a Gibson Les Paul are objects and they are under the electric guitar class.

In programming, you can call those guitars as instances of the class of objects named electric guitars. Each object has its own properties or characteristics.

Objects under the same class have same properties, but the value of those properties may differ or be the same per object. For example, think that an electric guitar's properties are: brand, number of strings, and number of guitar pickups.

Aside from that, each object has its own functions or things that it can do. When it comes to guitars, you can strum all the strings or you can just pick on one string.

If you convert that to Ruby code, that will appear as:

```
class ElectricGuitar
    def initialize
        @brand = "Local"
        @strings = 6
        @pickups = 3
    end
    def strum
        #Insert statements to execute when strum
is called
    end
    def pick
        #Insert statements to execute when strum
is called
end
```

Creating a Class

To create a class, you need to use the class keyword and an identifier. Class identifiers have the same syntax rules for constant identifiers. To end the creation of the class, you need to use the end keyword. For example:

```
irb(main):001:0> class Guitar
irb(main):002:1> end
=> nil
```

Creating an Object

Now, you have a class. It is time for you to create an object. To create one, all you need is to think of an identifier and assign the class name and the keyword new to it for it to become an object under a class. For example:

```
irb(main):001:0> fender = Guitar. new
=> #<Guitar:0x1234567>
```

Note: Do not forget to add a dot operator after the class name.

Unfortunately, the class Guitar does not contain anything in it. That object is still useless and cannot be used for anything. To make it useful, you need to add some methods and properties to it.

Methods

This is where it gets interesting. Methods allow your objects to have 'commands' of some sort. In case you want to have multiple lines of statements to be done, placing them under a class method is the best way to do that. To give your classes or objects methods, you will need to use the def (define) keyword. Below is an example:

```
irb(main):001:0> class Guitar
irb(main):002:1> def strum
irb(main):003:2> puts "Starts strumming."
irb(main):004:2> puts "Strumming."
irb(main):005:2> puts "Ends strumming."
irb(main):006:2> end
irb(main):007:1> end
=> :strum
```

Now, create a new object under that class.

```
irb(main):008:0> gibson = Guitar. new
=> #<Guitar:0x1234567>
```

To use the method you have created, all you need is to invoke it using the object. For example:

```
irb(main):009:0> gibson.strum
Starts strumming.
Strumming.
Ends strumming.
```

```
=> nil
```

By using the dot operator, you were able to invoke the method inside the gibson object under the Guitar class. All the objects that will be under Guitar class will be able to use that method.

Conclusion

Thank you again for purchasing this book!

I hope this book was able to help you understand how coding in Ruby works.

The next step is to:

- Learn more about flow control tools in Ruby
- Study about the other operators discussed in this book
- Research on how variables inside classes and objects work

Finally, if you enjoyed this book, please take the time to share your thoughts and post a review on Amazon. We do our best to reach out to readers and provide the best value we can. Your positive review will help us achieve that. It'd be greatly appreciated!

Thank you and good luck!

Check Out My Other Books

Below you'll find some of my other popular books that are popular on Amazon and Kindle as well. Simply click on the links below to check them out. Alternatively, you can visit my author page on Amazon to see other work done by me.

C Programming Success in a Day

Python Programming Success in a Day

PHP Programming Professional Made Easy

HTML Professional Programming Made Easy

CSS Programming Professional Made Easy

Windows 8 Tips for Beginners

C Programming Professional Made Easy

JavaScript Programming Made Easy

Rails Programming Professional Made Easy

Programming Box Set #77: Android Programming in a Day & Ruby Programming Professional Made Easy

C ++ Programming Success in a Day

If the links do not work, for whatever reason, you can simply search for these titles on the Amazon website to find them.